Century 21™
Computer Applications and Keyboarding

EIGHTH EDITION

Australia · Canada · Mexico · Singapore · Spain · United Kingdom · United States

Century 21™ E-Terms: A Dictionary for the 21st Century, Eighth Edition

Jack Hoggatt, Jon Shank

VP/Editorial Director:
Jack W. Calhoun

VP/Editor-in-Chief:
Karen Schmohe

Acquisitions Editor:
Jane Congdon

Project Manager:
Dave Lafferty

Consulting Editor:
Jean Findley,
Custom Editorial Productions, Inc.

VP/Director of Marketing:
Carol Volz

Marketing Manager:
Michael Cloran

Marketing Coordinator:
Linda Kuper

Senior Production Editor:
Martha Conway

Ancillary Coordinator:
Kelly Resch

Production Manager:
Tricia Boies

Senior Manufacturing Coordinator:
Charlene Taylor

Manager of Technology, Editorial:
Liz Prigge

Art Director:
Stacy Jenkins Shirley

Photography Manager:
Deanna Ettinger
John Hill

Permissions Editor:
Linda Ellis

Copyeditor:
Karen Davis

Production House:
Cadmus Professional Communications

Cover Designer:
Grannan Graphic Design, Ltd.

Cover Images:
© Getty Images, Inc.

Photo Researcher:
Deanna Ettinger

Printer:
West Group
Saint Paul, MN

ASIA (including India)
Thomson Learning
5 Shenton Way
#01-01 UIC Building
Singapore 068808

AUSTRALIA/NEW ZEALAND
Thomson Learning Australia
102 Dodds Street
Southbank, Victoria 3006
Australia

CANADA
Thomson Nelson
1120 Birchmount Road
Toronto, Ontario
Canada M1K 5G4

UK/EUROPE/MIDDLE EAST/AFRICA
Thomson Learning
High Holborn House
50-51 Bedford Road
London WC1R 4LR
United Kingdom

Table of Contents

-A-

A+ certification: certification and testing from CompTIA on skills for PC repair, computer hardware, and operating systems.

absolute cell reference: in spreadsheets, a reference to a cell or group of cells that does not adjust when the cell is copied or moved.

Access: a Microsoft application used to create a database.

active matrix: a term used to describe a high-quality display screen, such as those used on laptop computers.

adapter card: a generic term used to describe any card inserted onto the motherboard of a computer to add functions such as sound and video. Examples of adapter cards are those used to add modems and network connections to a computer.

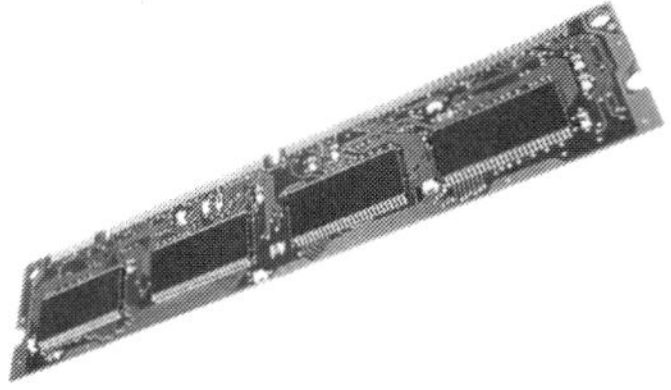

AIFF (Audio Interchange File Format): a sound file often used on Macintosh computers. The files can be quite large, so other formats are used more frequently.

Alt (Alternate) key: a keyboard option used in the Windows operating systems to provide additional functions for the alphanumeric keys. Just as the Shift+f produces a capital F, in Windows, selecting Alt+f drops down the file menu options. Not every Alt key combination produces a result, but learning keyboard shortcuts such as these speeds up the time needed to produce a document. Keyboard shortcuts can be found by looking to the right of a menu option.

animated GIF: a type of moving graphic used on web pages. If an arrow on a web page changes colors, shapes, rotation, or sizes, it is often an animated GIF.

animation: the process of adding graphics, visual effects, or sound to an object or text.

application: productivity software such as Microsoft Office. Applications are the programs a user accesses in order to produce a product or document.

"

ASCII (American Standard Code for Information Interchange): a standard means of transferring text from one user to another without having to be concerned about software compatibility. Files saved as ASCII text can be opened on any computer, although all formatting (such as columns and font choices) will be missing. To save a document as ASCII, a user chooses Save As and then selects *.txt. The .txt extension is an indication of ASCII.

AU (audio): a sound file similar to .wav.

auto-format: in a software application such as word processing, a feature that applies pre-determined formats to a block of text or as text is keyed.

AVI (Audio Video Interleaved): a popular format for video files.

baud rate: a measurement for the speed of data transmission.

beta version: an early version of a software program that is often provided to users to test for bugs before the program is marketed to the general public.

bidirectional: a term usually used with printers to indicate that information can flow in both directions at once. Modern printers often require bidirectional cables rather than older unidirectional ones. Use of a bidirectional printer or cable speeds up the printing process.

bit: the smallest unit of measurement used in defining computer memory. It is not a designation a user will often see. Eight bits is equal to one byte.

bitmap: a graphic created using pixels. Bitmaps represent the most common form of graphics and are used to produce digital photographs, scanned pictures, and pictures found on the Internet. Programs such as Adobe Photoshop and Windows Paint produce bitmaps. Bitmap graphics are considered paint documents rather than drawing documents, which use vector graphics.

BMP (bitmap): the extension for bitmap graphics. A bitmap is created using pixels and is considered a paint document.

Boolean operators: in a database or on the Web, words or symbols used for searching for information.

boot: the term used to describe the start-up of a computer. A user might be instructed to boot the computer, meaning to turn it on. To reboot a computer is to restart it.

bps (bits per second): the speed with which a modem can communicate with another computer. A 56K baud modem can connect at up to 56,000 bauds per second.

brick-and-mortar: a term used to differentiate between an Internet location and a physical one. A brick-and-mortar business is one that has a physical existence that can be visited. An Internet business is one that can only be visited electronically.

browser: the term used for Internet software that lets a user view web pages. Internet Explorer and Netscape are the two most common Internet browsers in use today.

bug: an error in computer software design that prevents it from working properly. A bug is often corrected when a software company releases a patch.

Bulletin Board System (BBS): an electronic message system that allows the posting of and responses to messages.

byte: the primary unit of measurement used in defining computer memory. It is used to describe both RAM and hard drive size. A kilobyte is 1 thousand bytes, a megabyte is 1 million bytes, a gigabyte is 1 billion bytes, and a terabyte is 1 trillion bytes.

C++: a computer language often used to write applications.

cache: a term to indicate the ability of a computer to store information that it knows the user will need shortly. It's like putting a raincoat in the front of a closet rather than the back when rain is forecast. The coat is still in storage, but it can be accessed quickly.

CAD (Computer-Aided Design): a means of creating architectural or mechanical designs using a computer.

Caps Lock: the keyboard function that locks all keys so they automatically key capital rather than lowercase letters. Caps Lock applies only to letters of the alphabet, not numbers and punctuation. A light on the keyboard generally indicates if Caps Lock is engaged.

Carpal Tunnel Syndrome: the name given to the compression of nerves in the wrist, causing pain, swelling, and the inability to use the hand. The syndrome falls into the category of repetitive stress disorder, and it is seen in workers who must use a keyboard or mouse for long periods of time. Rest, medical braces, and sometimes surgery are prescribed to relieve the symptoms, but the best medicine is prevention. Taking small, regular breaks from the computer is important. Use of wrist pads near the keyboard may also help. Proper keyboarding posture and careful attention to the height of the chair and desk are two ways to help avoid this painful injury.

CAT5 (Category 5): a type of cable  that has the ability to transfer information from one computer to another. CAT5 cables are frequently blue in color and indicate a network cable. They are also called twisted pair cables.

CD-ROM (Compact Disc-Read-Only Memory): the device used to read a CD (compact disc). Originally CDs were used to store music, but today they are also used to store computer programs because they have more storage capacity than a floppy disk. CD-ROMs now come in three versions: read-only (a true ROM), writable, and rewritable. Writable CD-ROMs allow the user to "burn," or create, a permanent CD. A rewritable CD works much like a floppy disk in that information can be added and removed.

cell: the box formed by the horizontal and vertical lines in a table or spreadsheet into which information is entered.

cell address: in a spreadsheet, the location of a cell as identified by the intersection of the column letter and the row number.

chat room: a means of providing a common message area for those users who log in to a specific site. Everyone can see and respond to the messages sent to a chat room, building a sense of community as visitors respond. Chat rooms are often identified according to interests, so a chat room might be limited, for example, to users with an interest in Civil War battles.

clip art: a generic term indicating a collection of graphic files. In earlier days, such art consisted of printed pages of pictures that could be cut out (clipped) and pasted onto a page. Today clip art is compiled into digital pages and can be inserted into a computer document.

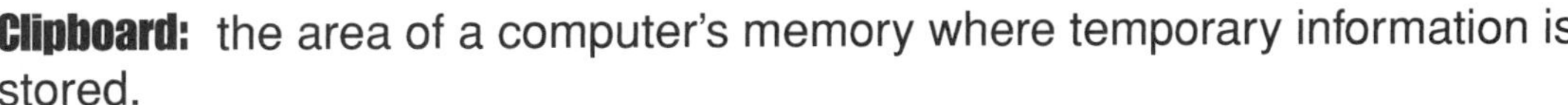

Clipboard: the area of a computer's memory where temporary information is stored.

close button: the X in the upper right corner of a window used to close a document or an application window.

compiler: for different programming languages such as Microsoft Visual Basic or Sun Microsystems Java, this is a software program used to run the listing of code.

computer: an electronic device that can perform tasks and calculations to provide logical information based on the instructions from the operator.

computer-assisted instruction: a means of delivering training using a computer. Its strength is that it can provide more repetition than instruction in an ordinary classroom and track a learner's successes and failures more easily.

cookie: a small piece of information stored on a user's computer designed to tell a web site that the user has visited that site before. It used to be of serious concern to computer users, but now most people accept it as a way of doing business on the Internet.

copyright law: legal restrictions against using another person's creative work. The law prohibits the copying of computer software for purposes other than archival (backup). This means one cannot "give" a copy of software to another person even if no payment is received.

CPU (Central Processing Unit): the "guts" of a computer. Users often refer to the "box" attached to the computer monitor as the CPU. The box actually contains far more than the CPU, but CPU is a convenient shortcut term. The CPU is actually the microprocessor, such as a Pentium, within the computer's case.

Ctrl (Control) key: a keyboard option used in application software to provide additional functions for the alphanumeric keys. Just as the Shift+f produces a capital F, in Microsoft Office, use of Ctrl+f opens up the Find/Replace box. Not every Ctrl key combination produces a result, but learning keyboard shortcuts such as these speeds up the time needed to produce a document. Keyboard shortcuts can be found by looking to the right of a menu option.

Ctrl-Alt-Delete: the keyboard action used to close an application that is not responding. A dialog box asking to end the task appears, allowing the user to exit the program. If a user's computer freezes or quits responding, Ctrl-Alt-Delete is a good method to recover use of the computer.

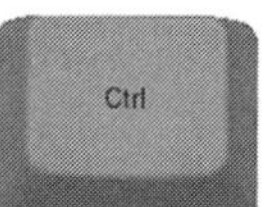

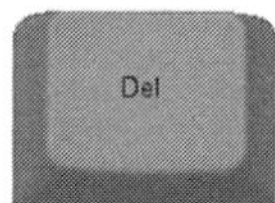

cut and paste: a way of copying or moving text or a graphic image by deleting the text or image from its original position in a file, placing it on the Clipboard, and then placing it in the desired software application.

-D-

data entry: a process of keying data or records in a software application.

data type: in a database, a classification of information, such as text, a date, currency, etc.

database: a computer application designed to store fields of information that can then be manipulated in many ways. A database is a powerful means of tracking all kinds of information. For example, a user might create a database with names, addresses, and phone numbers. That information can then be used to create mailing labels, record birthdays, or track telephone conversations.

denial of service: a term used to describe the loss of Internet service when computer hackers use a specially designed program to bombard a web site with messages, making it impossible for other users to access the site.

desktop: the primary screen of a Windows operating system. On it, a user will find My Computer, a recycling bin, and other shortcuts such as My Documents folder and Internet Explorer.

desktop publishing: the production of a document, usually incorporating both text and graphics. Originally, it indicated a difference in a publication created by a printing facility versus one created using a personal computer. In time, printers incorporated desktop publishing into their business, and the distinction disappeared.

dialog box: in a software application, this is a box that appears asking for a command or input from the user.

digital: a term used to describe the use of 0s and 1s (on/off) to create computer programs. Its antonym is *analog.* Today the term *digital* is often synonymous with *computer*, as in "the digital age."

digital camera: a camera that uses computer memory rather than film to store a photograph. Some digital cameras store pictures on floppy disks; others store them on flash or memory cards that are inserted into the camera as needed. The user can download the picture to a computer using a cable and an infrared port or by inserting the disk or flash card into the computer. Once the photograph is stored on the computer, it can be modified and printed. If a color printer and special glossy paper are used, the output can be near the quality of a film print.

dockable tool bar: a tool bar that can be moved from one location on the computer screen to another and then "locked" into place, usually at the top of the screen.

docking station: a means of converting a laptop computer to a desktop computer by "docking" it into special connections, providing the user with a standard keyboard, mouse, monitor, and perhaps network connection while using the laptop's CPU.

dongle: an attachment to a PC card that allows the user to connect to a network or telephone cable. It slips into the PC card using a small flat head and "dangles" outside the PC card waiting for the user to connect it to another cable. Be careful. It is easy to lose a dongle or to damage the head that attaches to the PC card. Dongles are usually designed for just one kind of PC card, so they are hard to replace if lost or damaged. Many new modem and network PC cards now have built-in connection ports, eliminating this problem.

dot com: a generic term covering Internet businesses since their addresses generally end in .com.

dot matrix printer: a type of printer that is used much less today than in years past. Dot matrix printers use a ribbon rather than a cartridge and produce documents by pressing each letter separately onto a page using a rotating head. They are slow and noisy, producing a document of lesser quality than ink-jet or laser.

dot pitch: a measurement of the closeness of the pixels on a monitor. The smaller the number, the better the picture. Dot pitch and resolution are the primary concern when choosing a monitor.

download: the process of moving software from the Internet to a computer. The most frequent downloads are from the Internet.

dpi (dots per inch): a type of measurement used with printers and scanners to indicate how many points of ink or pixels are contained in an inch. The more pixels and dots there are, the better the output or picture.

drag and drop: in word processing, a method for moving or copying text within a document.

DRAM: a type of high-quality RAM.

Dreamweaver: a software program from Macromedia that allows the user to create and manage web sites and Internet applications.

driver: software that is loaded onto a computer in order to run hardware such as a monitor, a modem, or a video card. It is usually provided by the manufacturer of the hardware, although operating systems such as Windows XP often contain a copy of the driver. It is also possible to download drivers from the Internet by going to the web site for the manufacturer of the hardware device and finding the driver download page.

drop-down menu: a listing of functions that appears when the user clicks on a word or an icon.

DSL (Digital Subscriber Line): a means of connecting to the Internet using regular telephone lines but without a modem. It is faster than using a modem but more expensive.

DVD (Digital Video Disc or Digital Versatile Disc): a disc similar in appearance to a CD but usually containing video or applications that require greater storage than a CD. DVD can be the disc or the player in which the disc is inserted.

-E-

e-book: a small device used to read text that has been downloaded into it. Several companies have designed e-books, but they have not been received enthusiastically by the general public, who seem to prefer paper versions instead. Originally the term *e-book* was limited to a hardware device, but some companies have developed e-readers that are used on a computer rather than as a separate reader. The result is that the term *e-book* has now come to mean the downloadable book file that can be purchased or is sometimes free. An interesting development was the introduction of a Stephen King book available only in e-book format. The future of e-books is still to be decided.

e-business: business conducted using the Internet that might be better called I-business. Web pages are an integral part of e-business as they offer a channel for advertising, sales, and information. E-commerce is another term used to describe the business of the Internet.

e-classes: instruction usually found on the Internet, but the term can also be used for computer-assisted instruction programs loaded onto the learner's computer.

e-learning: electronic version of brick-and-mortar education. E-learning can be used to develop skills for a particular industry, such as MOS certification for office workers, or to earn a college diploma.

e-mail: the modern equivalent of sending a letter using the Internet rather than the postal service. The address of the recipient (such as user@isp.net) is entered into the "To" line, and the subject is keyed into the "Subject" line. The body of the message is keyed into the open box below.

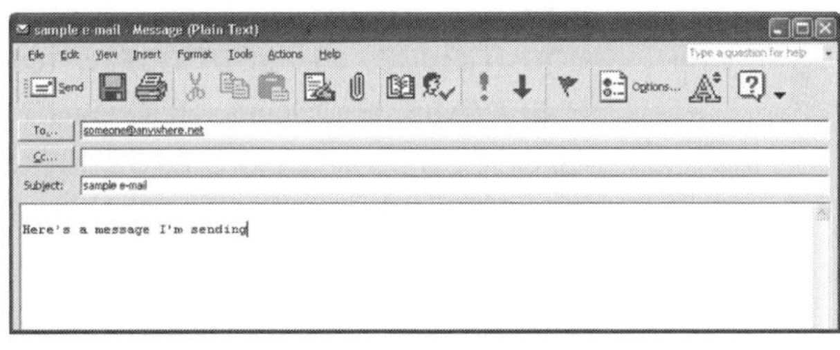

e-mail attachment: a document attached to an e-mail, often using a paper clip icon. The recipient of the document receives the document in exactly the same form that it was sent, so a spreadsheet will arrive as a spreadsheet and can be read and used in a spreadsheet program. If it's important that the information retain its original use, sending the document as an attachment is quite useful.

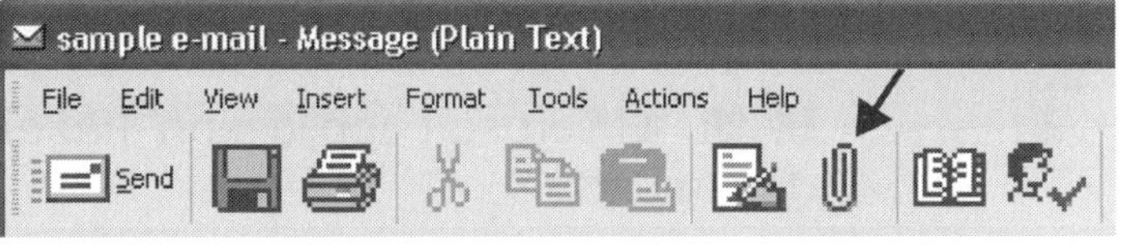

e-mail group: the gathering together of a group of e-mail addresses that have something in common. Using a group to send an e-mail means that the user only has to select one address to send everyone in the group the same message. It is an important means of increasing e-mail productivity.

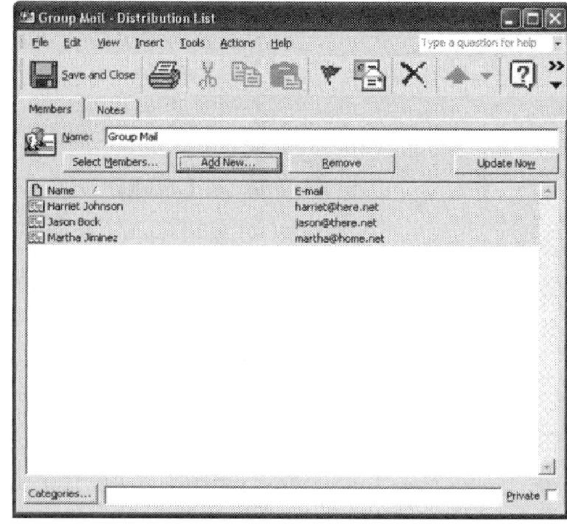

emoticon: a drawing created with keyboard letters and symbols. The most common is a smiley face produced using a colon and a right parenthesis :) Microsoft Word can take this series of keystrokes and replace it with an actual picture.

e-paper: electronic paper designed to be written on and "erased" as often as necessary. Erasing is achieved by redistributing the electrons on the page, much like shaking an Etch-A-Sketch to remove a drawing.

ergonomics: the study of how the body works in order to design better tools. The goal of ergonomics is to create tools such as chairs, desks, and pens to prevent injury while increasing productivity. Ergonomics is not limited just to offices. It may also include items such as home appliances that need to be designed to facilitate their proper use. Whether to place the controls of an oven on the front or top of the appliance is an ergonomic question.

e-term: a word that has been modified to indicate its entry into the electronic age (hence, *e*). Common e-terms include *e-learning, e-business, e-mail, e-schools, e-books,* and even *e-paper*. It's a shortcut that quickly identifies the new focus for an old product. Some people have complained that e-terms have become so prevalent that they have lost their impact.

Ethernet: a means of connecting computers together over a network. An Ethernet card is an adapter card that uses Ethernet as the means of moving information from one computer to another. There are other types of network cards, but Ethernet is the one most commonly used today.

Excel: a Microsoft application that allows a user to create spreadsheet documents.

extension: the three-letter addition to the name of a file indicating the type of application that produced the document. For example, Word documents end in .doc and Excel documents end in .xls.

FAQ (Frequently Asked Questions): a list of questions that is often included in software documentation or on a web site to answer questions that occur frequently. FAQs are the first place to look for information, since other users may have already encountered the same problem.

field: a grouping of similar information often used in databases. For example, in a database containing information about customers, a field might be account representatives or telephone numbers.

file server: see *server.*

firewall: a means of blocking outside users from having network access to computers within a system. Firewalls are used to protect networked computers from destructive actions by users outside the system.

FireWire: a connection to a computer similar to USB or a parallel port that allows the rapid exchange of information between a computer and the device attached to it. Both USB and FireWire are more modern connection ports than serial and parallel.

Fireworks: a software program from Macromedia that allows the user to design and optimize web graphics for integration into a web site.

flame: strong or harsh words used in e-mail, often as a result of some offense the original sender has committed. To flame another person is the equivalent of cursing at them and is to be discouraged. Often flaming is taken more seriously than the sender intends and can lead to a series of flame wars.

flash card: an insert into a digital camera to be used as storage for photographs taken with the camera.

floating tool bar: a tool bar that can be detached from its original (or docked) location and moved to one more convenient for the user.

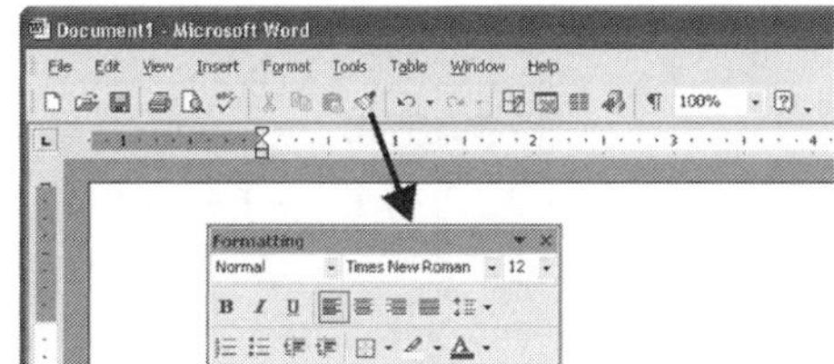

floppy disk: a means of storing a small amount of information permanently in a portable format. A floppy stores 1.44 megabytes of information, which makes it much smaller than a hard drive, but it can be removed easily to move from computer to computer. The floppy drive is frequently labeled the "A:" drive. A user can determine how much storage space is left on a floppy disk by following these steps:

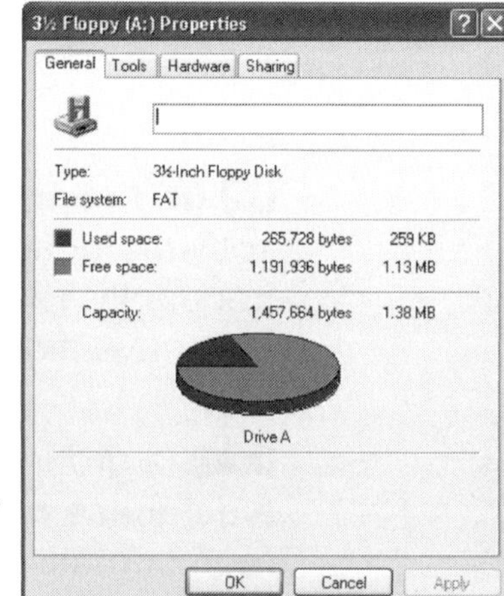

1. Insert the floppy into the computer.

2. Double click the My Computer icon on the desktop.

3. Right click on the A: drive icon.

4. Choose Properties. A circle graph shows how much space is used and how much is free.

floppy drive: the device into which a floppy disk is inserted. Today's floppy drives use 3½-inch disks with hard plastic covers. In earlier years, floppy drives used 5¼-inch disks with soft plastic covers, but these are now obsolete.

formula: in a spreadsheet, an equation or instruction to calculate data using cell references and ranges.

frames: sections of a web page that can be formatted, sized, and made to scroll.

FreeHand: a software program from Macromedia that allows the user to create and print vector-based illustrations for the Web.

freeware: software provided free to users. It is usually downloadable from special Internet sites that gather together software for that purpose. Often a computer programmer will offer a program as freeware to see if there is enough interest to develop a full-featured version that is marketable. Freeware may have bugs (or errors), making it difficult to use, or it may be an excellent addition to a user's computer. Programs (such as Internet browsers) that are offered free from major computer companies in order to build or keep a large body of users are generally not described as freeware.

FrontPage: a Microsoft application that allows a user to create web pages.

FTP (File Transfer Protocol): a means of sending files by way of the Internet, requiring the user to use FTP software.

function: in a spreadsheet, an automatic formula that performs calculations such as SUM or AVG.

function keys: keys found across the top of the computer keyboard labeled F1, F2, and so on. They are frequently used as shortcuts in computer programs. In Microsoft Word, for example, pressing the F7 key opens the spell-checking function.

-G-

GB (gigabyte): a measurement of size generally for hard drives. Drives were originally measured in kilobytes (K), then megabytes (MB or 1,000 K), and now gigabytes (1,000 MB or 1,000,000 K). The term is often abbreviated *gig,* as in a 10-gig drive.

GHZ (gigahertz): a measurement of processor speed. A processor that functions in gigahertz is very powerful since some processors today are still rated in megahertz.

GIF (Graphic Interchange Format): the extension for a graphic file that is often used for line drawings requiring few colors. GIF graphics are viewable using Internet browsers.

GPS (Global Positioning System): a hardware device that uses satellite technology to provide information about a user's exact location in the world.

graphic: a picture, photograph, drawing, or captured picture such as a scanned document. Graphic files have various extensions, each indicating the type of program used to create them. The most common are .jpg, .gif, and .png (all able to be used on web pages), as well as .bmp, .tif, and .pcx.

groupware: software programs that allow people on a network to work together remotely.

gutter: the space between columns in a multicolumn document. Microsoft Word also uses *gutter* to mean the binding space along the left side of a page.

-H-

hard drive: a small metal box located within a computer on which to store computer information permanently. It is referred to as memory, such as RAM and ROM, but actually has less to do with the computer's processing and more to do with its square footage of storage. It is measured in megabytes (MB) or gigabytes (GB). The hard drive is frequently labeled the "C:" drive. A user can determine how much storage space is left on a hard drive by following these steps:

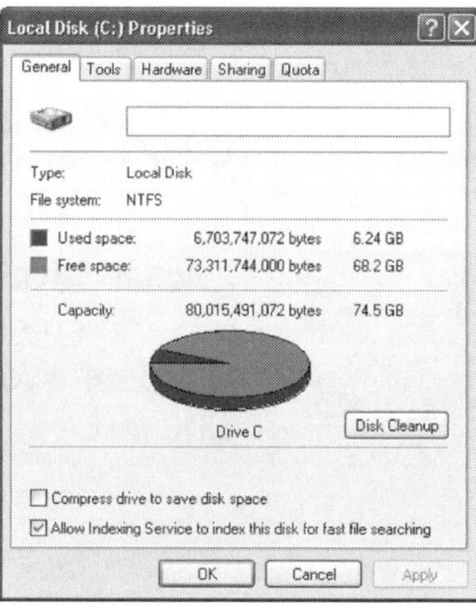

1. Double click the My Computer icon on the desktop.

2. Right click on the C: drive icon.

3. Choose Properties. A circle graph shows how much space is used and how much is free.

hardware: the components of a computer system, such as the keyboard, hard drive, and printer. Its antonym is *software*.

header/footer: the space at the top or bottom of a document where recurring information is listed, such as a page number. Each page in a document will usually have the same header or footer information.

help desk: computer user support for technical issues and operations.

home page: the starting page of a web site.

HTML (Hypertext Markup Language): the code used to create a web page. This term is sometimes used as a synonym for a web page.

HTTP (Hypertext Transfer Protocol): the opening letters keyed in a web address (URL) that tell the browser that the user is searching for a web page. In years past, a user needed to key http:// before entering the rest of the address, but today the browser usually enters it automatically.

hub: a hardware box into which several computers are plugged using a network cable (often blue). A hub allows computers to communicate with each other.

hyperlink: an Internet link to another web page or to another location within a web page. It is usually indicated by blue text with a blue underline, but it can also be a button or graphic. The cursor changes to a hand with a pointing finger as it passes over the hyperlink. Clicking on the link takes the user to a new location.

hypermedia: the combination of hypertext and multimedia on a web page, creating a page with both text and action.

hypertext: text on a web page that is linked to another web page or to another location within a web page. It is usually indicated by blue text with a blue underline until it has been selected once. Once a hypertext link has been used, it will change colors, usually to a reddish pink color.

icon: a small graphic used to identify a computer function such as a program or a feature. Clicking on an icon for a floppy disk will open the disk. Clicking on a tool bar icon will open an application feature.

IEEE: a special type of bidirectional cable designed to work best with modern printers.

IMAP (Internet Message Access Protocol): information that may be required to set up an e-mail account. It indicates what type of server is managing a user's e-mail. The other choice is usually POP3. The provider of the e-mail service supplies this information.

infrared port: a component of a computer, frequently a laptop, that allows the computer to communicate with another device, such as a printer, using a beam of light rather than a physical cable.

ink-jet printer: a type of printer that "squirts" ink onto a page, forming letters and graphics. Ink-jet printers are less expensive than laser printers while providing a high-quality printout. Such printers also have color capabilities, making them ideal for graphic work. The drawback is that supply costs for the replacement ink cartridges are proportionally more expensive than laser cartridges.

Instant Messenger: an e-mail program developed by AOL that allows users to communicate in real time, meaning that as soon as one person keys an instant message, the recipient receives it. The advantage of Instant Messenger over standard e-mail is the immediacy of the message.

integration: for software applications such as word processing and spreadsheet, this is the ability to share data; for example, using part of a spreadsheet in a word processing document.

Intel: a company that produces many of the microprocessors used in personal computers. Pentium processors are produced by Intel.

Internet: the interconnecting of computers in many locations. Originally the Internet was accessed using different methods, but today it is largely limited to browsers searching the World Wide Web (hence, many Internet addresses begin with www). Today the Internet is generally synonymous with the Web.

Internet Explorer: an Internet browser developed by Microsoft.

Internet filter: a means of preventing a user from having access to certain sites on the Internet. It is generally used to block pornographic or violent sites from viewing by children.

intranet: a network within an organization that allows users to communicate with members of the organization without concern that users outside the organization can observe the flow of information. Only those within the organization's network can view an intranet web site. It is protected from outsiders by a firewall.

IP (Internet Protocol): the numeric address of a computer connected to the Internet consisting of four sets of numbers separated by periods, such as 131.183.113.159. An IP address is similar to a street address in that it tells the network server how to find the computer. The IP address is set by choosing Network properties from the Control Panel. Some computers have static IP addresses, meaning they never change. Other Internet providers assign a dynamic IP when the user logs on, so no IP is necessary.

ISDN (Integrated Services Digital Network): a means of using phone lines to transfer computer information quickly. Its features are similar to a modem connection but faster and more expensive.

ISP (Internet Service Provider): a service that provides users with e-mail and Internet accounts that can be accessed using either a modem or a network connection. Generally, an ISP charges a fee for providing this access. A user's e-mail address identifies the provider in the information following the @ symbol (user@ISP.NET).

IT (Information Technology): a term used to indicate those who oversee technology and the transfer of information using technology, as in "The IT department is sending someone to load new software."

JavaScript: a computer script that increases functionality of web pages. For example, a JavaScript added to the HTML code on a web page might change the picture of a red arrow to a green one when a user clicks on the arrow, or it might send a user to a new web page if the current one is unavailable.

JavaScript error: an error message that may appear when a web page opens, indicating that the JavaScript code used to create special actions by the page designer is not functioning correctly. It is harmless to click the OK button. Generally, a user will not notice any loss of information. It does not indicate any problem with the user's computer.

JPEG or JPG (Joint Photographic Experts Group): an extension indicating a graphic file that works best with photographs using many colors. JPEGs are one kind of graphic that can be viewed on a web page.

K (kilobyte): 1,000 bytes. A kilobyte is a measurement of storage and memory capacity of a computer or disk. A floppy disk can store 1.44 kilobytes. A hard drive might store as much as a million kilobytes or more.

keyboard shortcut: a means of accessing program features without using the mouse for clicking on menus or toolbars. Shortcuts usually require the use of the Alt key, Ctrl key, or function keys. Learning to use keyboard shortcuts is a means of increasing productivity, because it is not necessary to stop keying in order to activate functions such as spell checking; the user's hands do not have to leave the keyboard. Keyboard shortcuts are listed to the right of menu functions on the menu bar.

-L-

LAN (Local Area Network): the joining together of computers within a small area (such as a building) using a network connection.

LAN party: a group of game players who use a network installed specifically for the event.

laptop computer: a notebook or portable computer.

laser printer: a type of printer that functions on the same principle as a photocopy machine, using a toner cartridge and heat to seal the toner on the page. Laser printers are more expensive than ink-jet printers, but their printing cost per page is significantly less than ink-jet. While there are color laser printers, they are quite expensive. Most users of laser printers do not use them for color output. Their advantage, other than cost, is speed of printing and quality of output.

LCD (Liquid Crystal Display): a means of displaying an image on a monitor using a special crystal. This type of display is often used on laptop computers and flat panel monitors.

license: permission granted by the creator of software to the purchaser to use the software. A software license does not usually confer ownership. The terms of the contract that the user accepts when buying software vary from company to company. However, most software companies retain ownership of the software (but not the media on which it is recorded, such as a CD or disk), so the license proves right of use.

line break: the separation of text to a new line.

link: see *hyperlink.*

linking: the process of connecting data between files so that a change in one will automatically cause a change in the other.

Linux: an operating system software from Sun MicroSystems, Inc., that supports the Java programming language.

list serve: a form of e-mail that allows a message to be sent to more than one user.

log in: the process of keying a name and perhaps a password to gain permission to enter a network or get into an Internet site, as in "to log in with your password." To log out is to close the connection.

log on: the process of connecting to a network, as in "logging on to the Internet." To log off is to leave the network.

-M-

Macromedia Studio Suite: a set of software programs from Macromedia that consists of Flash, Dreamweaver, Fireworks, and FreeHand.

mail merge: a means of combining a list of information, such as names and addresses, into a master document and then producing multiple documents using this information. For example, a user's address book could be mail merged into a holiday letter, personalizing the letter for each person who receives it. Mail merge is often used to create mailing labels as well as form letters.

mainframe: a large computer that is capable of processing and storing large amounts of information.

maximize button: the button that increases the size of the window of a document so it fills the screen. Once the screen covers the page, the button changes to a restore button that can be toggled to reduce the size of the window.

MB (megabyte): a million bytes. It is used to measure storage and memory capacity. RAM memory sticks might have 16 MB of memory capacity. A hard drive might have 400 MB of storage memory. The term is often abbreviated *meg*, as in 32 megs of memory.

MBPS (megabytes per second): a measurement of network card speed. Cards are rated at 10 or 100 MBPS, although many will be listed as 10/100, meaning they can function at either speed depending upon the hub they are attached to.

Media Player: a Windows utility program that allows the user to play sound and video files.

menu bar: a listing of functions within a particular application available to a user. The bar is usually located across the top of the screen.

MHZ (megahertz): a measurement of speed used to describe how fast a computer can process information. A modern computer might be rated at 800 megahertz, while an older one might be rated at 16. A Pentium 650 would be a computer with a Pentium processor running at 650 megahertz.

microprocessor: see *processor.*

MIDI or MID (Musical Instrument Digital Interface): a sound file extension usually indicating a musical recording but not voice. Musical keyboards that can be attached to a computer to record music are called midi boards.

minimize button: the button that sends the document window to the task bar. The window is no longer visible on the screen, but the document is still open.

modem: a hardware device used to connect one computer to another using a telephone line. Modems can be located internally on an adapter card found within the computer or externally in a box attached to the computer. In both cases, a telephone line is connected to an RJ11 port, similar to the connections found on telephones. Modern modems can connect to the Internet at a maximum speed of 56K bps (bits per second), but many phone lines do not actually connect the user at the maximum speed possible.

monitor: a peripheral hardware device that allows the computer user to view software applications and data.

MOS (Microsoft Office Specialist): a set of tests designed to evaluate a user's ability to create documents using Microsoft Office applications.

motherboard: the main board in a computer that operates the computer. On it is located the microprocessor and other components necessary to make a computer "think." Most users do not worry about the motherboard in their computer; instead, they are concerned with the processor and its speed.

mouse: a hand-held peripheral device that allows input and operation of the computer via a pointer on the screen.

MP3 (MPEG Layer-3 Audio): a digital sound file that is copied from a CD and compressed, making it easier and faster to download from the Internet. Copying of MP3 files has been the subject of considerable discussion within the music industry, since distributing the files to other users can be a violation of copyright laws.

MPEG or MPG (Moving Picture Experts Group): the extension for video files that display movies. They can be quite large and may require considerable time to download from the Internet.

multimedia: the use of graphics, sound, and video in a single document, such as a web page.

-N-

netiquette: the rules of e-mail and Internet usage. For example, netiquette requires that a user key text using upper- and lowercase letters rather than all capital letters because the use of all caps is viewed as shouting.

Netscape: an Internet browser. Its main competition is Internet Explorer.

network: the means of connecting one computer to another whether both computers are in the same room or in different countries. The Internet is a giant network. Generally, computers are networked by attaching a cable (often blue) from a network adapter within the computer to a box called a hub. From this hub, another cable runs to a router that directs the computer's message to other computers. A modem can be used to connect a computer to a network using a telephone line.

NIC (Network Interface Card): a common term used for a network card.

non-system disk error: an error message that usually means a floppy disk has been left in the computer when it was turned off. Removing the disk and striking a key will continue the start-up of the computer.

notebook computer: see *laptop computer.*

Novell: software used to connect network computers.

Num Lock: the keyboard term for having the numeric keypad activated. A light on the keyboard generally indicates if Num Lock is engaged. Most computers automatically engage Num Lock when they boot.

-O-

OCR (Optical Character Recognition): a means of converting a scanned document into text using a software package. The letter A, when it is scanned, is saved as a graphic or picture. OCR software can "read" the graphic A and convert it to a text letter A.

Office: a group of Microsoft applications that includes word processing (Word), database (Access), spreadsheet (Excel), and presentation (PowerPoint) software, as well as others, depending upon the package choices.

offline: a term used in a printer environment to mean that the printer is not turned on, is not working, or is not connected to the computer. When accessing a network, offline means that the connection is turned off. It is possible to use e-mail software offline, meaning that the user can compose a message without being connected by a modem to an ISP. Once the message is completed, the user connects or goes online to send it.

online: the status that indicates a computer is connected to the Internet and is ready to receive or transmit data.

operating system: the software program, such as Windows XP, that runs a computer. It differs from application software, such as Microsoft Office, which is productivity software. Users often confuse operating system functions with the functions of productivity software. An operating system allows the user to do things such as save files, load software, and find applications. A program allows the user to produce a document.

orientation: the vertical or horizontal placement of a document when it is printed. Portrait orientation is vertical placement, while landscape is horizontal.

Outlook: a Microsoft product that functions as a personal organizer with e-mail, a calendar, an address book, and other functions. Outlook is part of the Microsoft Office package.

Outlook Express: an e-mail software application that comes with the installation of Internet Explorer. It is not the same product as Outlook.

-P-

PageMaker: a software program from Adobe that allows the user to perform desktop publishing functions to create different documents.

Palm Pilot: a brand of personal digital assistant; one of the first PDAs on the market and still the industry standard. See *PDA*.

parallel: a method of sending information between a computer and another hardware device such as a printer. A parallel printer connects to the parallel port on the back of the computer. Parallel devices are faster than serial ones because multiple lines of information are sent at one time, unlike serial devices that send information in a single line.

patch: an update to computer software designed to fix a flaw in the original program.

path: the location of a document stored in a computer's hard drive, on a floppy disk, or on another storage device. A document's path might be C:/my docs/letters/Franklin. This path would indicate that a document was stored in the C: drive in the folder (directory) "my docs." Within that folder is nested another folder called "letters" and a file within called "Franklin." In other words, the letter to Franklin is stored four layers down.

PC (Personal Computer): a term often used to distinguish between a Macintosh (Mac) and an IBM-compatible computer, as in "Are you using a Mac or a PC?"

PC repair: the study of methods to fix and build computer hardware components and operating systems.

PCMCIA (PC card): a credit-card-size piece of hardware used to add functions to a laptop computer. PC cards are generally used to add a modem or network connection to a laptop, but they may also be used to add capabilities such as hard drive storage capacity (an "extra closet" in which to store information). PC cards are inserted into an open slot, usually on the side of a laptop.

PCX (Paintbrush): the extension for a bitmap graphic created using Paint, a Windows utility program.

PDA (Personal Digital Assistant): a small hand-held computerlike device designed to store information such as a calendar and an address book. PDAs started out as replacements for paper data organizers such as Day-Timers, but have become more full-featured. Many of them now offer Internet and e-mail access as well as other enhancements.

PDF (Portable Document Format): the extension for a file created by an Adobe software product called Acrobat that comes in two parts: a free document reader and software with which to create PDF documents. A PDF reader can be downloaded free from the Adobe web page and installed on a user's computer in order to read any files created with this program. PDF files, which retain all formatting and images, have become common on Internet sites as a means of providing multipage, complex documents without having to worry if a user has the necessary software to read them. As such, PDF files are becoming a universal means of delivery.

peer-to-peer: a networking system that connects one computer to another without the use of a server to store information. Information is passed directly from one peer (computer) to another peer.

Pentium: a brand of microprocessor created by Intel that is currently the industry standard. Pentium processors are numbered, with the Pentium 5 being the newest on the market. The 286 (80286), 386, and 486 were the precursors of the Pentium.

peripherals: the various external hardware parts and components of a computer system, such as the monitor, printer, scanner, speakers, disk drives, etc.

Photoshop: a software program from Adobe that allows the user to create and edit graphics to use with desktop publishing.

piracy: the stealing of software by copying it and giving or selling it to another person. A computer pirate may be a "businessperson" who is making copies to sell to a large number of users, or it may be someone who is sharing software with friends. In either case, computer piracy is illegal, and a person can be subject to legal penalties if these actions are discovered by the software company. Copying information, graphics, and sounds from the Internet can also fall into the category of piracy if that information is used for publication.

pixel (picture element): a small square used to create a graphic. Different colored pixels are combined to form the picture one sees. If a drawing is enlarged too much, it becomes "pixilated," meaning the pixels become visible as jagged edges.

plug-in: an additional feature added to an Internet browser. Plug-ins are usually downloaded free from the Internet. One of the most common plug-ins is Shockwave.

POP3 (Post Office Protocol): information that may be required to set up an e-mail account. It indicates what type of server is managing a user's e-mail. An e-mail server may be a POP3 or IMAP type. The provider of the e-mail service supplies this information.

PowerPoint: a Microsoft application that allows users to create presentation documents used to display and enhance the flow of information, such as while giving a speech.

PPM (Pages Per Minute): a measurement of the number of pages a printer can produce in a minute. The number is dependent upon the graphics on a page and the amount of color used, so it can be subjective.

presentation software: a program such as PowerPoint that allows the user to create a series of slides for showing concepts and ideas to others.

processor: the primary brain of a computer. A processor's speed and capabilities are the most significant descriptor of a computer's capabilities. Early processors included the 80286 (called a 286), 80386, and 80486. Today's processors include Pentiums, Celerons, and others. Different manufacturers, such as Intel and AMD, identify similar processors with different names. Processors are ranked according to brand and speed. Speeds are measured as megahertz. Faster is better.

program: a general term used to describe any action performed by a computer. Operating systems and application software are both programs.

programming: the process of creating computer code using a computer language.

protocol: the standards and rules for two or more computers to communicate with each other.

proxy server: an intermediary between a user and the Internet. A proxy can filter requests for web pages, denying access to those sites selected by the administrator of the server. Use of a proxy can also speed up access to web information by storing pages most often requested so they can be accessed quickly.

Publisher: a software program from Microsoft that allows the user to perform desktop publishing functions to create different documents.

-Q-

Quark XPress: a software program from Quark, Inc., that allows the user to perform desktop publishing functions to create different documents.

query: a selection of database information based upon predetermined criteria. For example, a query might select all records that contain zip codes within a certain range.

Quicken: a software application that allows the user to track expenses and income, much like a checkbook.

-R-

RA (Real Audio): the extension for a sound file that can only be heard using Real Audio, a sound program that can be downloaded from the Internet.

RAM (Random-Access Memory): temporary memory used by a computer to store information currently being used by the computer. As soon as the computer is turned off, the information disappears. In human terms, it is similar to short-term memory. For example, if a person observes clouds floating by, that person will not remember later the cloud patterns that passed unless he or she saves a picture by photographing the clouds. In this same way, a computer stores information for the long term by saving to a permanent source such as a floppy disk or hard drive. RAM is sold on small "sticks" slightly larger than a piece of gum. RAM can be increased by adding additional sticks to the computer. RAM is measured in kilobytes (K) ranging from as few as 8 to as many as 256 (or more). The more RAM a computer has, the more it can retain in short-term memory.

record: a complete set of single entries into a database field. For example, a record listing client information might include entries into the fields for name, address, and telephone number.

relational database: a database that can work with two or more files at one time.

relative cell reference: in spreadsheets, this is a reference to a cell or group of cells that adjusts when the cell is copied or moved.

Repetitive Stress Disorder: a category of physical injuries suffered by workers who must repeat the same task over a long period of time. Carpal Tunnel Syndrome is one of the most common, but injuries may also be to the elbow, eyes, and any part of the body exposed to the constant motion. Even eyestrain can fall into this category. Workers can avoid eyestrain by blinking frequently and developing the habit of refocusing on objects at a distance from the computer screen. Joint injury to workers is less likely if they take breaks at regular intervals. Utility programs can be added to computers that are designed to interrupt work and remind the user to take a break.

resolution: an indicator of how many pixels are used to create a picture. The number may be used to describe a monitor's resolution, a photograph created with a digital camera, or a picture copied using a scanner. A monitor resolution can be set at 640X480 pixels, 800X600 pixels, 1024X768 pixels, or greater. Graphic resolutions fall into similar categories.

restore button: the button used to reduce the size of the window of a document so it does not fill the entire computer screen. The size can be changed by "pushing" or "pulling" the screen using the diagonal bars in the lower right corner of the window (Macintosh) or by dragging one of the window's edges or corners (PC). To return the window to a larger size, the user clicks the maximize button.

right click: the use of the right mouse button to access special features of a PC application. For example, using Microsoft Word, right clicking on a word underlined in red will drop down a list of possible spelling options.

rip: the process of copying a song from a CD in order to transfer it to a computer or another device. To rip a CD is to convert all the music on the disc to an MP3 format.

ROM (Read-Only Memory): data on a computer that has been prerecorded and cannot change; permanent memory used by a computer in order for it to know how to function as soon as it is turned on. In human terms, it is similar to long-term memory, such as a person's ability to always remember his or her name. It is measured in kilobytes (K).

router: a hardware box that routes network traffic from one location to another, ensuring that e-mail sent to a specific address gets to the proper server and that a web site is sent to the user requesting that page.

scanner: a device that converts a document to a digital image. Once the image is created, users can modify it using graphic software or convert it to a text document using OCR software. Flatbed scanners are the most common, requiring the user to lift a lid and place the document on a glass plate, much like using a photocopy machine. Sheetfed scanners allow the user to feed the material in, much like rolling paper into a typewriter.

scroll bar: a means of moving a page vertically or horizontally using arrows or the "elevator" box. Scroll bars on the right side control the vertical movement. Bars at the bottom control horizontal movement.

SDRAM: a type of RAM memory that is faster than earlier versions.

search engine: an Internet function that allows the user to search the Internet for specific sites related to the terms entered. Common search engines are Yahoo, Alta Vista, and Excite. Metasearch engines combine results from all the major search engines. Because the Internet is so large, it is important to learn the tools needed to refine searches before they occur. Two important tools are the use of quotes around terms to ensure that the search engine is seeking that exact term. For example, keying the term "War of 1812" will limit the search to just that war. Without the quotation marks, the engine will search for the actual war as well as war in general and the date 1812. A second technique is to use a plus before a word to ensure that the word must appear or to use a minus to eliminate words that the user does not want to appear. Keying +"War of 1812" and +"New Orleans" will ensure that both items appear on the web pages before being listed as finds.

security: the process of restricting access to data and applications on a computer or network.

serial: a method of sending information between a computer and another hardware device such as a mouse. A serial device connects to a serial port on the back of the computer. Serial devices are slower than parallel ones because single lines of information are sent at one time, unlike parallel devices that send information in multiple lines.

server: a computer used to store information for more than one computer user and provide access to common files. In order for users to access a server from their own computer, special software is often required, such as that provided by Novell. "The server is down" means that the server computer has been taken out of service or is not working.

shareware: software provided to users on a trial basis. Once a user decides to keep the software, the user sends payment to the developer of the software. It is an excellent method of evaluating software on a "try before you buy" plan.

sharing: a means of providing access to a computer's files or printer over a network so others can read or use them. Shared files can be set for "read only," meaning other users cannot change them. Files can also be set to allow other users complete control of the document, letting them make any changes they want.

Shockwave: an addition or plug-in to an Internet browser that allows the user to see multimedia created with Macromedia's Director. Shockwave can be downloaded free from the Internet, which makes it possible to view the special effects found on web pages with Shockwave features.

shortcut: a Microsoft Windows feature that directs the operating system to a particular location. Shortcuts are usually identified with an arrow. Clicking on one opens an application or a document just as if it were the original. The difference is that removing a shortcut does not remove the application or document. Think of it as a road sign indicating a direction to the town ahead. Removing the sign does not remove the town. A user can create a shortcut in a number of ways, including right clicking on the original document or application and selecting "make a shortcut." Once the shortcut has been created, the user can move it anywhere on the desktop.

shrink wrap license: the software license that is invoked as soon as the plastic wrapping is removed from a new software package. Accepting a shrink wrap license means the user automatically agrees to the terms of the contract between the user and the computer company as soon as the seal is broken or the software is used.

slides: the pages created in presentation software such as PowerPoint that comprise the structure of a presentation.

Smart Tags: in Microsoft Office, a set of buttons that are common in function in the different applications, such as Word and Excel.

SMTP (Simple Mail Transport Protocol): information needed to send e-mail. The e-mail provider can supply this information.

snail mail: a somewhat humorous description of postal mail.

software: a general term used to describe computer programs such as applications and operating systems.

sound card: an adapter card inserted into slots on a motherboard, allowing the user to hear sound played through the computer. Sound cards are usually required if a user has a CD-ROM installed on a computer. More powerful sound cards give better sound and can be replaced easily if necessary. Many motherboards come with a built-in sound card, meaning that no additional card is necessary.

sound file: a file that can produce sound on a computer. Special recording software is used to produce sound files; the result may have an extension such as .wav, .mp3, or .mid.

spam: unsolicited e-mail that is frequently used as a sales technique. It is the equivalent of telemarketing phone calls one receives at dinnertime.

spreadsheet: a computer program that begins as a series of cells created using vertical and horizontal lines. These cells are filled with information (often numerical) and then manipulated with tools provided by the spreadsheet application. For example, a list of expenses could be entered into cells and then a formula entered into the last cell to add up the total expenses.

SSL (Secure Sockets Layer): a means of providing security on the Internet for information sent from one user to another. Sites that have addresses beginning with *https* are using SSL and are considered secure.

streaming: a means of seeing video or hearing sound files as soon as they are sent from a web site. Use of streaming means that the sound or video will load faster and play as soon as the information first appears.

supercomputer: the fastest, most advanced type of computer; used to store vast amounts of data and perform many complex tasks.

surge suppressor: a device designed to protect a computer system from a power surge, as might occur during an electrical storm. Some surge suppressors provide more protection than others, generally based upon price. Surge suppressors usually have several outlets on a power strip, but not all power strips have surge suppressor capabilities.

system software: see *operating system.*

-T-

T-1: a fast network connection provided as a leased line, meaning that it is not part of a standard telephone connection.

tablet PC: a form of laptop or notebook computer that acts as a writing tablet, where the user can translate handwritten notes into electronic text.

task bar: a bar, usually at the bottom of the screen, that indicates what documents are currently open on the desktop. Clicking on a document on the task bar opens the document window or makes it the "top" window. The task bar can be moved to other locations by dragging it.

TCP/IP (Transmission Control Protocol/Internet Protocol): a protocol that the computer uses to access the Internet. The TCP information tells the computer which gate to use to get onto the network and which server is providing the service. This information is supplied by the administrator of the network or the Internet service provider.

telecommunications: a form of communication that uses electronic devices such as a computer, telephone, modem, telephone lines, or satellites.

terabyte: a billion kilobytes or a million megabytes or a thousand gigabytes of information. A very large hard drive might have a terabyte of storage space.

TFT (Thin Film Transistor): a technology equivalent to active matrix; used to describe high-quality displays, such as those available for laptop computer screens.

tool bar: a grouping of icons that  provides the most commonly used functions of an application. A tool bar is usually at the top of the Windows screen directly below the menu bar. Many programs allow the user to select what icons to include in the tool bar. More than one tool bar can be open at once.

transparent GIF: a graphic file that allows the background of the picture to be invisible. It is used most often on web pages to give the impression that the picture is embedded in the background.

Trojan horse: a destructive program similar to a virus.

-U-

unzip: a process of opening a file that requires using an unzip program such as WinZip. Unzip programs can be downloaded from the Internet as freeware or shareware. Once the program is loaded onto a computer, double clicking on a file with a .zip extension will uncompress, or open up, all the documents saved within the zipped file. Depending upon the unzip program being used, the user must determine where to extract the uncompressed files and then save them. Once they have been saved, the user can access all the files that have been "zipped" into the single file by opening the folder to which the files have been extracted.

upload: the process of moving software from a computer to the Internet or a server, as in "I uploaded a copy of my file to the server."

UPS (Uninterruptible Power Supply): a device designed to provide temporary power to a computer system in the event that electrical power is lost.

URL (Uniform Resource Locator): the technical name for a web-site address.

USB (Universal Serial Bus): a method of sending information between a computer and another hardware device such as a mouse or a printer. A USB device connects to a USB port on the back of the computer. USB devices are faster than parallel or serial devices and have the added advantage of allowing the user to attach the device while the computer is on. In addition, multiple devices can be attached through a single USB port. Currently USB devices are replacing both serial and parallel ones.

-V-

vector graphic: a graphic created using mathematical formulas to draw lines. While a bitmap graphic creates a picture using small squares, a vector graphic creates a drawing with a series of lines (straight or curved). Vector graphics can be resized without losing clarity. A drawing program such as Corel Draw is used to create vectors.

video card: an adapter card inserted into a slot on a motherboard, allowing the user to attach a monitor to the computer. Video cards with more RAM can display better graphics on a monitor and rebuild the picture faster, making programs such as games appear to run faster. Video cards can be replaced if necessary. Many motherboards come with built-in video cards.

virtual reality: a computer program that shows a simulated environment that appears to be three-dimensional in its use of graphics.

virus: software that changes a user's computer without the user's permission or knowledge. It is usually passed on to an unsuspecting user by way of the Internet, by e-mail, or by using disks infected with the virus. E-mail files that have attachments such as .exe files are often a means of sending viruses, although viruses have also been attached to word processing documents. Several companies provide virus protection software, such as Norton Antivirus and McAfee, but new viruses are created daily. It is necessary to update virus protection frequently in order to protect a computer from infection. Most virus software companies offer free Internet updates for owners of their programs.

Visual Basic: a computer language from Microsoft that is used to write software applications.

voice recognition: a software package that can convert digital sound into text, much like OCR software converts scanned documents into text. Popular voice recognition software includes Dragon NaturallySpeaking and ViaVoice.

VRAM (Video RAM): the amount of memory found on a video card. More RAM means that the graphics on a monitor appear more quickly.

-W-

WAN (Wide Area Network): the joining together of computers over a large area, such as from one building to another, using a network connection. The distinction between LAN and WAN is no longer as important as it once was since more and more computers are joined to the Internet (a giant WAN).

WAV (Windows Audio Volume): a basic sound file that can be read by computers with Windows operating systems. WAV files are often quite large, and other, smaller sound files are often used for Internet transfer.

web address: the information needed to access a web page on the Internet. A web address written as www.nameofcompany.com indicates three things: that this is a World Wide Web address (now common but not always the case in years past), what the name of the company is, and that it is a commercial site (.com). Other common extensions are .edu (education), .gov (government), .mil (military), .net (network), and .org (nonprofit organization). Newer extensions such as .biz (business) have recently been added.

web browser: a software application that allows a web page to display information retrieved from the Internet, such as Internet Explorer.

web design: the process of creating a web site using application software such as FrontPage or Dreamweaver.

web page: a single page of information accessed through the Internet. It is created using HTML code and is usually linked to other pages. It may contain text as well as graphics, sound, and video.

web site: a grouping of web pages under a single name. For example, a web site for South-Western (www.swlearning.com) contains many web pages of information about textbooks, all linked to a common web-site address.

webmaster: the person who oversees the creation and management of a web page or web site.

Windows: an operating system created by the Microsoft Corporation. The versions of Windows are numbered or lettered, with Windows 3.11 being followed by Windows 95, Windows 98, Windows 2000, and Windows XP. Windows 3.11 is quite different from the later versions of Windows. With the advent of Windows 95, the look of the desktop and the means of accessing functions, such as opening and finding files, changed dramatically.

wireless: a means of connecting one computer to another using transmission through the air. It does not require a physical connection between computers and a hub or switch.

wizard: a pre-designed template that allows the user to create documents in a certain format; a series of tasks that are linked together to simplify the process of creating a document or installing software. For example, a mail-merge wizard guides the users through all the steps needed to create a mail-merged letter. Wizards are also used to load software onto a computer, either requiring the user to click on the setup icon found on the disk or having a self-loading CD appear on screen.

Word: a Microsoft application that allows a user to create word processing documents.

word processing: a software application that allows the user to key text and then manipulate it. Word processors allow the user to check spelling, change font size and type, modify margins, set tabs, and create columns. Modern word processing software has gone well beyond these basic tasks, letting users insert tables or charts, change color of text, and add graphic elements.

word wrap: the automatic continuation of keyed text down to the next line. Users have come to expect that the software will recognize the end of a line and continue text on the next line.

Works: a Microsoft product that provides basic word processing, spreadsheet, and database capabilities in a single application. It is easy to confuse the names Works and Word. Word is word processing software included in Office. Works is a multifunction package often used when more powerful software is not needed.

worksheet: another term for spreadsheet; it contains rows and columns that intersect to form a grid for creating documents with calculations.

worm: a type of virus.

write-protect tab: a movable slide found in the upper right corner of a floppy disk. When the window it covers is open, no changes can be made to the information stored on the disk, so it is write-protected. Usually, the slide is closed, allowing the user to make changes. If one turns the floppy disk over, a graphic of an open and closed lock may be located on the back,

providing a key to the purpose of each position. When saving information to a floppy disk, if an error message appears saying that the disk is write-protected, check to see if the slide has been dislodged slightly from its usual position. It should click into the unprotect position.

WWW (World Wide Web): the first three letters that appear in a web address, notifying the Internet that the user is seeking a web site rather than some other Internet site, such as FTP.

WYSIWYG (What You See Is What You Get): an acronym meaning that what appears on the screen is what will be printed. While this is common today, in the early years of personal computers, that was not the case; users had to guess how their documents would appear, particularly in regard to line breaks. The phrase one might encounter is "This program is totally WYSIWYG," meaning that the user will know what to expect when the document is printed.

-Z-

Zip disk: a disk similar to a floppy disk except that it is slightly larger and can store nearly 100 times as much information as a floppy disk. Zip disks are very useful if one needs to transport large files, such as those created using graphics and sound.

Zip drive: a device similar to a floppy drive except that it requires a Zip disk. A Zip drive may be internal, meaning it is located in a bay of the computer just like a floppy drive, or it may be in an external box attached to the computer. Unlike floppy drives that are generic and produced by several manufacturers, a single company, Iomega, markets Zip drives.

Zip file: a document that has been compressed to take up less space on a computer and to make it quicker to download over the Internet. It can be identified by the extension .zip (such as filename.zip). Often Zip files contain more than a single file. Once the original file has been uncompressed, or opened up, these files are extracted to a new location. To use a Zip file, a user must uncompress it using a special unzip file such as WinZip or PKUnzip. If a computer does not have an unzip program, one can be downloaded from the Internet and installed on the computer. Do not confuse a Zip file with a Zip drive. A Zip drive is a piece of hardware, similar to a floppy disk drive; a Zip file is a computer file.

Directions: Match the terms to the definitions below by writing in the correct term.

e-mail	emoticon	Instant Messenger	SMTP
e-mail attachment	flame	list serve	snail mail
e-mail group	IMAP	POP3	spam

_______________________ 1. a document attached to an e-mail, often using a paper clip icon

_______________________ 2. a drawing created with keyboard letters and symbols

_______________________ 3. a somewhat humorous description of postal mail

_______________________ 4. an e-mail program that allows users to communicate in real time, meaning that as soon as one person keys a message, the recipient receives it

_______________________ 5. information needed to send e-mail

_______________________ 6. Post Office Protocol

_______________________ 7. Internet Message Access Protocol

_______________________ 8. strong or harsh words used in e-mail, often as a result of some offense the original sender has committed

_______________________ 9. the gathering together of a group of e-mail addresses that have something in common

_______________________ 10. the modern equivalent of a letter using the Internet rather than the postal service

_______________________ 11. unsolicited e-mail that is frequently used as a sales technique

_______________________ 12. a form of e-mail that allows a message to be sent to more than one user

✓ E-Term Quick Check ✓

Directions: Match the terms to the definitions below by writing in the correct term.

e-book	**e-learning**	**e-term**	**online**
e-business	**e-paper**	**IT**	**telecommunications**
e-classes			

_______________________   1. a small device used to read text that has been downloaded into it

_______________________   2. a term used to indicate those who oversee technology and the transfer of information using technology

_______________________   3. a word that has been modified to indicate its entry into the electronic age

_______________________   4. business conducted using the Internet that might be better called I-business

_______________________   5. electronic paper designed to be written on and "erased" as often as necessary

_______________________   6. electronic version of brick-and-mortar education

_______________________   7. information technology

_______________________   8. instruction usually found on the Internet, but the term can also be used for computer-assisted instruction programs loaded onto the learner's computer

_______________________   9. the status that indicates a computer is connected to the Internet and is ready to receive or transmit data

_______________________   10. a form of communication that uses electronic devices such as a computer, telephone, modem, telephone lines, or satellites

✓ Hardware Quick Check ✓

Directions: Match the terms to the definitions below by writing in the correct term.

adapter card	floppy drive	modem	scanner
Caps Lock	GPS	monitor	SDRAM
CAT5	hard drive	motherboard	server
CD-ROM	hardware	mouse	sound card
computer	hub	NIC	supercomputer
CPU	IEEE	Num Lock	surge suppressor
docking station	infrared port	Palm Pilot	tablet PC
dongle	ink-jet printer	PCMCIA	UPS
dot matrix printer	Intel	PDA	video card
DRAM	laptop computer	Pentium	VRAM
DVD	laser printer	peripherals	write-protect tab
FireWire	mainframe	processor	Zip disk
flash card	microprocessor	router	Zip drive
floppy disk			

_________________________ 1. a brand of microprocessor that is currently the industry standard

_________________________ 2. a common term used for a network card

_________________________ 3. a company that produces many of the microprocessors used in personal computers

_________________________ 4. a component of a computer, frequently a laptop, that allows the computer to communicate with another device using a beam of light

_________________________ 5. a computer used to store information for more than one computer user

_________________________ 6. a connection to a computer similar to USB or a parallel port that allows the rapid exchange of information between a computer and the device attached to it

_________________________ 7. a credit-card-size piece of hardware used to add functions to a laptop computer

_________________________ 8. a device designed to protect a computer system from a power surge, as might occur during an electrical storm

_________________________ 9. a device designed to provide temporary power to a computer system in the event that electrical power is lost

_________________________ 10. a device similar to a floppy drive except that it requires a Zip disk

_________________________ 11. a device that converts a document to a digital image

_________________________ 12. a disc similar in appearance to a CD but usually containing video or applications that require greater storage than a CD

13. a disk similar to a floppy disk except that it is slightly larger and can store nearly 100 times as much information as a floppy disk

14. a generic term used to describe any card inserted onto the motherboard of a computer to add functions such as sound and video

15. a hardware box into which several computers are plugged using a network cable

16. a hardware box that routes network traffic from one location to another

17. a hardware device that uses satellite technology to provide information about a user's exact location in the world

18. a hardware device used to connect one computer to another using a telephone line

19. a means of converting a laptop computer to a desktop computer by "docking" it into special connections

20. a means of storing a small amount of information permanently, in a portable format

21. a movable slide found in the upper right corner of a floppy disk

22. a small hand-held computerlike device designed to store information such as a calendar and an address book

23. a small metal box located within a computer on which to store computer information permanently

24. a special type of bidirectional cable designed to work best with modern printers

25. a type of cable that has the ability to transfer information from one computer to another

26. a type of high-quality RAM

27. a type of printer that "squirts" ink onto a page, forming letters and graphics

28. a type of printer that functions on the same principle as a photocopy machine, using a toner cartridge and heat to seal the toner on the page

29. a type of printer that is used much less today than in years past

30. a type of RAM memory that is faster than earlier versions

31. an adapter card inserted into a slot on a motherboard, allowing the user to attach a monitor to the computer

32. an adapter card inserted into slots on a motherboard, allowing the user to hear sound played through the computer

33. an attachment to a PC card that allows the user to connect to a network or telephone cable

34. an insert into a digital camera to be used as storage for photographs taken with the camera

35. Global Positioning System

36. one of the first PDAs on the market

37. the "guts" of a computer

38. the amount of memory found on a video card

39. the components of a computer system, such as the keyboard, hard drive, and printer

40. the device into which a floppy disk is inserted

41. the device used to read a CD

42. the keyboard function that locks all keys so they automatically key capital rather than lowercase letters

43. the keyboard term for having the numeric keypad activated

44. the main board in a computer that operates the computer

45. the primary brain of a computer

46. an electronic device that can perform tasks and calculations to provide logical information based on the instructions from the operator

47. a notebook or portable computer

48. a large computer that is capable of processing and storing large amounts of information

49. a peripheral hardware device that allows the computer user to view software applications and data

50. a hand-held peripheral device that allows input and operation of the computer via a pointer on the screen

51. the various external hardware parts and components of a computer system, such as the monitor, printer, scanner, speakers, disk drives, etc.

52. the fastest, most advanced type of computer; used to store vast amounts of data and perform many complex tasks

53. a form of laptop or notebook computer that acts as a writing tablet, where the user can translate handwritten notes into electronic text

✓ Internet Quick Check ✓

Directions: Match the terms to the definitions below by writing in the correct term.

brick-and-mortar	**HTML**	**LAN party**	**upload**
browser	**HTTP**	**log in**	**URL**
Bulletin Board	**hyperlink**	**log on**	**virus**
System (BBS)	**hypermedia**	**netiquette**	**web address**
chat room	**hypertext**	**Netscape**	**web browser**
cookie	**Internet**	**plug-in**	**web design**
denial of service	**Internet Explorer**	**search engine**	**web page**
dot com	**Internet filter**	**Shockwave**	**web site**
download	**intranet**	**SSL**	**webmaster**
frames	**ISP**	**streaming**	**worm**
FTP	**JavaScript**	**Trojan horse**	**WWW**
home page	**JavaScript error**		

_______________________ 1. a computer script that increases functionality of web pages

_______________________ 2. a destructive program similar to a virus

_______________________ 3. a generic term covering Internet businesses since their addresses generally end in .com

_______________________ 4. a group of game players who use a network installed specifically for the event

_______________________ 5. a grouping of web pages under a single name

_______________________ 6. a means of preventing a user from having access to certain sites on the Internet

_______________________ 7. a means of providing a common message area for those users who log in to a specific site

_______________________ 8. a means of providing security on the Internet for information sent from one user to another

_______________________ 9. a means of seeing video or hearing sound files as soon as they are sent from a web site

_______________________ 10. a means of sending files by way of the Internet, requiring the user to use FTP software

_______________________ 11. a message that may appear when a web page opens if the code used by the designer of the page to create special actions is not functioning correctly

_______________________ 12. a network within an organization that allows users to communicate with members of the organization without concern that users outside the organization can observe the flow of information

_______________________ 13. an electronic message system that allows posting of and responses
    to messages

_______________________ 14. a service that provides users with e-mail and Internet accounts that
    can be accessed using either a modem or a network connection

_______________________ 15. a single page of information accessed through the Internet

_______________________ 16. a small piece of information stored on a user's computer designed
    to tell a web site that the user has visited that site before

_______________________ 17. a synonym for a web page, although it is actually the code used to
    create a web page

_______________________ 18. a term used to describe the loss of Internet service when computer
    hackers bombard a web site with messages, making it impossible
    for other users to access the site

_______________________ 19. a term used to differentiate between an Internet location and a
    physical one

_______________________ 20. a type of virus

_______________________ 21. an addition or plug-in to an Internet browser that allows the user to
    see multimedia created with Macromedia's Director

_______________________ 22. an additional feature added to an Internet browser

_______________________ 23. an Internet browser developed by Microsoft

_______________________ 24. an Internet browser

_______________________ 25. an Internet function that allows the user to search the Internet for
    specific sites related to the terms entered

_______________________ 26. an Internet link to another web page or to another location within a
    web page

_______________________ 27. Hypertext Markup Language

_______________________ 28. printed information that is linked to a web page

_______________________ 29. software that changes a user's computer without the user's
    permission or knowledge

_______________________ 30. the combination of hypertext and multimedia on a web page,
    creating a page with both text and action

_______________________ 31. the first three letters that appear in a web address, notifying the
    Internet that the user is seeking a web site rather than some other
    Internet site, such as FTP

_______________________ 32. the information needed to access a web page on the Internet

_______________________ 33. the interconnecting of computers in many locations

34. the opening letters keyed in a web address that tell the computer that the user is searching for a web page

35. the person who oversees the creation and management of a web page or web site

36. the process of connecting to a network

37. the process of keying a name and perhaps a password to gain permission to enter a network or get into an Internet site

38. the process of moving software from a computer to the Internet or a server

39. the process of moving software from the Internet to a computer

40. the rules of e-mail and Internet usage

41. the starting page of a web site

42. the technical name for a web-site address

43. the term used for Internet software that lets a user view web pages

44. sections of a web page that can be formatted, sized, and made to scroll

45. a software application that allows a web page to display information retrieved from the Internet, such as Internet Explorer

46. the process of creating a web site using application software such as FrontPage or Dreamweaver

 # Multimedia Quick Check 

Directions: Match the terms to the definitions below by writing in the correct term.

AIFF	Dreamweaver	MIDI or MID	RA
animated GIF	Fireworks	MP3	rip
animation	Freehand	MPEG or MPG	sound file
AU	GIF	multimedia	transparent GIF
AVI	graphic	PCX	vector graphic
bitmap	JPEG or JPG	Photoshop	virtual reality
BMP	Macromedia Studio	pixel	WAV
clip art	Suite		
digital camera	Media Player		

____________________ 1. a basic sound file that can be read by computers with Windows operating systems; these files are often quite large

____________________ 2. a camera that uses computer memory rather than film to store a photograph

____________________ 3. the process of adding graphics, visual effects, or sound to an object or text

____________________ 4. a digital sound file that is copied from a CD and compressed, making it easier and faster to download from the Internet

____________________ 5. a file that can produce sound on a computer

____________________ 6. a generic term indicating a collection of graphic files

____________________ 7. a graphic created using mathematical formulas to draw lines

____________________ 8. a software program from Macromedia that allows the user to create and manage web sites and Internet applications

____________________ 9. a graphic created using pixels

____________________ 10. a graphic file that allows the background of the picture to be invisible

____________________ 11. a picture, photograph, drawing, or captured picture such as a scanned document

____________________ 12. a software program from Macromedia that allows the user to design and optimize web graphics for integration into a web site

____________________ 13. a popular format for video files

____________________ 14. a small square used to create a graphic

____________________ 15. a sound file extension usually indicating a musical recording but not voice

____________________ 16. a software program from Macromedia that allows the user to create and print vector-based illustrations for the Web

_______________________ 17. a sound file often used on Macintosh computers

_______________________ 18. a sound file similar to .wav

_______________________ 19. a type of moving graphic used on web pages

_______________________ 20. a set of software programs from Macromedia that consists of Flash, Dreamweaver, Fireworks, and FreeHand

_______________________ 21. a Windows utility program that allows the user to play sound and video files

_______________________ 22. an Adobe application that allows a user to create and modify graphics

_______________________ 23. an extension indicating a graphic file that works best with photographs using many colors

_______________________ 24. a computer program that shows a simulated environment that appears to be three-dimensional in its use of graphics

_______________________ 25. Musical Instrument Digital Interface

_______________________ 26. the extension for a bitmap graphic created using Paint, a Windows utility program

_______________________ 27. the extension for a graphic file that is often used for line drawings requiring few colors

_______________________ 28. the extension for a sound file that can only be heard using Real Audio, a sound program downloaded from the Internet

_______________________ 29. the extension for bitmap graphics

_______________________ 30. the extension for video files that display movies

_______________________ 31. the process of copying a song from a CD in order to transfer it to a computer or another device

_______________________ 32. the use of graphics, sound, and video in a single document, such as a web page

Directions: Match the terms to the definitions below by writing in the correct term.

absolute cell	data type	MOS	record
reference	database	Novell	relational database
Access	desktop publishing	OCR	relative cell
application	drag and drop	Office	reference
ASCII	Excel	orientation	shareware
auto-format	extension	Outlook	shrink wrap license
beta version	FAQ	Outlook Express	slides
Boolean operators	field	PageMaker	software
bug	formula	PDF	spreadsheet
C++	freeware	piracy	unzip
CAD	FrontPage	PowerPoint	voice recognition
cell	functions	presentation	Word
cell address	groupware	software	word processing
computer-assisted	gutter	program	word wrap
instruction	header/footer	Publisher	Works
copyright law	license	Quark XPress	worksheet
cut and paste	line break	query	WYSIWYG
data entry	mail merge	Quicken	Zip file

____________________ 1. a complete set of single entries into a database field

____________________ 2. a computer application designed to store fields of information that can then be manipulated in many ways

____________________ 3. in spreadsheets, a reference to a cell or group of cells that does not adjust when the cell is copied or moved

____________________ 4. a computer language often used to write applications

____________________ 5. a computer program that begins as a series of cells created using vertical and horizontal lines

____________________ 6. a document that has been compressed to take up less space on a computer and to make it quicker to download over the Internet

____________________ 7. in a software application such as word processing, a feature that applies pre-determined formats to a block of text or as text is keyed

____________________ 8. a general term used to describe any action performed by a computer

____________________ 9. a general term used to describe computer programs such as applications and operating systems

____________________ 10. a group of Microsoft applications that includes word processing (Word), database (Access), spreadsheet (Excel), and presentation (PowerPoint) software, as well as others, depending upon the package choices

11. a grouping of similar information often used in databases

12. in a database or on the Web, words or symbols used for searching for information

13. in a spreadsheet, the location of a cell as identified by the intersection of the column letter and the row number

14. a list of questions that is often included in software documentation to answer questions that occur frequently

15. a means of combining a list of information into a master document and then producing multiple documents using this information

16. a means of converting a scanned document into text using a software package

17. a way of copying or moving text or a graphic image by deleting the text or image from its original position in a file, placing it on the Clipboard, and then placing it in the desired software application

18. a process of keying data or records in a software application

19. a means of creating architectural or mechanical designs using a computer

20. a means of delivering training using a computer

21. a Microsoft application that allows a user to create presentation documents used to display information

22. a Microsoft application that allows a user to create spreadsheet documents

23. in a database, a classification of information, such as text, a date, currency, etc.

24. a Microsoft application that allows a user to create web pages

25. a Microsoft application that allows a user to create word processing documents

26. a Microsoft application that provides basic word processing, spreadsheet, and database capabilities in a single application

27. in word processing, a method for moving or copying text within a document

28. in a spreadsheet, an equation or instruction to calculate data using cell references and ranges

29. a Microsoft application used to create a database

30. a Microsoft product that functions as a personal organizer with e-mail, a calendar, an address book, and other functions

_______________________ 31. a process of opening a file that requires using an unzip program such as WinZip

_______________________ 32. a selection of database information based upon predetermined criteria

_______________________ 33. in a spreadsheet, an automatic formula that performs calculations such as SUM or AVG

_______________________ 34. software programs that allow people on a network to work together remotely

_______________________ 35. a software application that allows the user to key text and then manipulate it

_______________________ 36. a software application that allows the user to track expenses and income, much like a checkbook

_______________________ 37. a software package that can convert digital sound into text, much like OCR software converts scanned documents into text

_______________________ 38. a standard means of transferring text from one user to another without having to be concerned about software compatibility

_______________________ 39. a software program from Adobe that allows the user to perform desktop publishing functions to create different documents

_______________________ 40. a program such as PowerPoint that allows the user to create a series of slides for showing concepts and ideas to others

_______________________ 41. a set of tests designed to evaluate a user's ability to create documents using Microsoft Office applications.

_______________________ 42. American Standard Code for Information Interchange

_______________________ 43. an acronym meaning that what appears on the screen is what will be printed

_______________________ 44. an Adobe software product that comes in two parts: a free reader and a software product with which to create PDF documents

_______________________ 45. a software program from Microsoft that allows the user to perform desktop publishing functions to create different documents

_______________________ 46. an early version of a software program that is often provided to users to test for bugs before the program is marketed to the general public

_______________________ 47. an e-mail software application that comes with the installation of Internet Explorer

_______________________ 48. a software program from Quark, Inc., that allows the user to perform desktop publishing functions to create different documents

_______________________ 49. an error in computer software design that prevents it from working properly

_______________________ 50. legal restrictions against using another person's creative work

_______________________ 51. a database that can work with two or more files at one time

_______________________ 52. permission to use software, not ownership

_______________________ 53. productivity software such as Microsoft Office

_______________________ 54. software provided free to users

_______________________ 55. in spreadsheets, a reference to a cell or group of cells that adjusts when the cell is copied or moved

_______________________ 56. the pages created in presentation software such as PowerPoint that comprise the structure of a presentation

_______________________ 57. another term for spreadsheet; it contains rows and columns that intersect to form a grid for creating documents with calculations

_______________________ 58. software provided to users on a trial basis

_______________________ 59. software used to connect network computers

_______________________ 60. the automatic moving of keyed text down to the next line

_______________________ 61. the box formed by the horizontal and vertical lines in a table or spreadsheet into which information is entered

_______________________ 62. the production of a document, usually incorporating both text and graphics

_______________________ 63. the separation of text to a new page

_______________________ 64. the software license that is invoked as soon as the plastic wrapping is removed from a new software package

_______________________ 65. the space at the top or bottom of a document where recurring information is listed, such as a page number

_______________________ 66. the space between columns in a multicolumn document

_______________________ 67. the stealing of software by copying it and giving or selling it to another person

_______________________ 68. the three-letter addition to the name of a file indicating the type of application that produced the document

_______________________ 69. the vertical and horizontal placement of a document when it is printed

✓ Technical Quick Check ✓

Directions: Match the terms to the definitions below by writing in the correct term.

A+ certification	Ethernet	network	resolution
active matrix	firewall	non-system disk	ROM
baud rate	GB	error	security
bidirectional	GHZ	offline	serial
bit	help desk	parallel	T-1
boot	IP	patch	TCP/IP
bps	ISDN	PC	terabyte
byte	K	PC repair	TFT
cache	LAN	peer-to-peer	USB
compiler	LCD	PPM	Visual Basic
digital	Linux	programming	WAN
dot pitch	MB	protocol	wireless
dpi	MBPS	proxy server	
DSL	MHZ	RAM	

_____________________ 1. a billion kilobytes or a million megabytes or a thousand gigabytes of information

_____________________ 2. a fast network connection provided as a leased line, meaning that it is not part of a standard telephone connection

_____________________ 3. a means of blocking outside users from having network access to computers within a system

_____________________ 4. a means of connecting computers together over a network

_____________________ 5. a means of connecting one computer to another using transmission through the air

_____________________ 6. a means of connecting to the Internet using regular telephone lines but without a modem

_____________________ 7. a means of displaying an image on a monitor using a special crystal

_____________________ 8. a means of using phone lines to transfer computer information quickly, similar to a modem connection

_____________________ 9. a measurement of network card speed

_____________________ 10. a measurement of processor speed

_____________________ 11. a measurement of size generally for hard drives

_____________________ 12. a measurement of speed used to describe how fast a computer can process information

_____________________ 13. a measurement of the closeness of the pixels on a monitor

14. a measurement of the number of pages a printer can produce in a minute

15. a method of sending information between a computer and another hardware device such as a mouse or a printer; faster than parallel or serial devices, with the added advantage of allowing the user to attach the device while the computer is on

16. a method of sending information between a computer and another hardware device such as a mouse, with single lines of communication sent at one time

17. a method of sending information between a computer and another hardware device such as a printer, with multiple lines of information sent at one time

18. a million bytes

19. a networking system that connects one computer to another without the use of a server to store information

20. a protocol that the computer uses to access the Internet

21. a technology equivalent to active matrix used to describe high-quality displays, such as those available for laptop computer screens

22. a term often used to distinguish an IBM-compatible computer from a Macintosh computer

23. a term to indicate the ability of a computer to store information that it knows the user will need shortly

24. a term used in a printer environment to mean that the printer is not turned on, is not working, or is not connected to the computer

25. a term used to describe a high-quality display screen, such as those used on laptop computers

26. a term used to describe the use of 0s and 1s

27. a term usually used with printers to indicate that information can flow in both directions at once

28. a type of measurement used with printers and scanners to indicate how many points of ink or pixels are contained in an inch

29. an error message that usually means a floppy disk has been left in the computer when it was turned off

30. an indicator of how many pixels are used to create a picture

31. an intermediary between a user and the Internet

32. an update to computer software designed to fix a flaw in the original program

33. local area network

_______________________ 34. 1,000 bytes

_______________________ 35. permanent memory used by a computer in order for it to know how to function as soon as it is turned on

_______________________ 36. temporary memory used by a computer to store information currently being used by the computer

_______________________ 37. the joining together of computers over a large area, such as from one building to another, using a network connection

_______________________ 38. the joining together of computers within a small area using a network connection

_______________________ 39. the means of connecting one computer to another whether both computers are in the same room or in different countries

_______________________ 40. the numeric address of a computer connected to the Internet consisting of four sets of numbers separated by periods, such as 131.183.113.159

_______________________ 41. the primary unit of measurement used in defining computer memory

_______________________ 42. the smallest unit of measurement used in defining computer memory

_______________________ 43. the speed with which a modem can communicate with another computer

_______________________ 44. the term used to describe the start-up of a computer

_______________________ 45. certification and testing from CompTIA on skills for PC repair, computer hardware, and operating systems

_______________________ 46. a measurement for the speed of data transmission

_______________________ 47. for different programming languages such as Microsoft Visual Basic or Sun Microsystems Java, this is a software program used to run the listing of code

_______________________ 48. computer user support for technical issues and operations

_______________________ 49. an operating system software from Sun MicroSystems, Inc., that supports the Java programming language

_______________________ 50. the study of methods to fix and build computer hardware components and operating systems

_______________________ 51. the process of creating computer code using a computer language

_______________________ 52. the standards and rules for two or more computers to communicate with each other

_______________________ 53. the process of restricting access to data and applications on a computer or network

_______________________ 54. a computer language from Microsoft that is used to write software applications

✓ Windows Quick Check ✓

Directions: Match the terms to the definitions below by writing in the correct term.

Alt key	**driver**	**maximize button**	**sharing**
Clipboard	**drop-down menu**	**menu bar**	**shortcut**
close button	**floating tool bar**	**minimize button**	**Smart Tags**
Ctrl key	**function keys**	**operating system**	**task bar**
Ctrl-Alt-Delete	**icon**	**path**	**tool bar**
desktop	**integration**	**restore button**	**Windows**
dialog box	**keyboard shortcut**	**right click**	**wizard**
dockable tool bar	**linking**	**scroll bar**	

_______________________ 1. a bar, usually at the bottom of the screen, that indicates what documents are currently open on the desktop

_______________________ 2. a graphic used to identify a computer function such as a program or a feature

_______________________ 3. a grouping of icons that provides the most commonly used functions of an application

_______________________ 4. a keyboard option used in application software to provide additional functions for the alphanumeric keys

_______________________ 5. a keyboard option used in the Windows operating systems to provide additional functions for the alphanumeric keys

_______________________ 6. a listing of the functions within a particular application that are available to a user

_______________________ 7. a listing of functions that appears when the user clicks on a word or an icon

_______________________ 8. a means of accessing program features without using menus or tool bars; usually requires the use of the Alt key, Ctrl key, or function keys

_______________________ 9. a means of moving a page vertically or horizontally using arrows or the "elevator" box

_______________________ 10. a means of providing access to a computer's files or printer over a network so others can read or use them

_______________________ 11. a Microsoft Windows feature that directs the operating system to a particular location

_______________________ 12. a series of tasks that are linked together to simplify the process of creating a document or installing software

_______________________ 13. a tool bar that can be detached from its original location and moved to one more convenient for the user

_______________________ 14. a tool bar that can be moved from one location on the computer
                             screen to another and then "locked" into place, usually at the top of
                             the screen

_______________________ 15. an operating system created by the Microsoft Corporation

_______________________ 16. Control key

_______________________ 17. keys found across the top of the computer labeled F1, F2, and so
                             on

_______________________ 18. software that is loaded onto a computer in order to run hardware
                             such as a monitor, a modem, or a video card

_______________________ 19. the button that increases the size of the window of a document so it
                             fills the screen

_______________________ 20. the button that sends the document window to the task bar

_______________________ 21. the button used to reduce the size of the window of a document so
                             it does not fill the entire computer screen

_______________________ 22. the keyboard action used to close an application that is not
                             responding

_______________________ 23. the location of a document stored in a computer's hard drive, on a
                             floppy disk, or on another storage device

_______________________ 24. the primary screen of a Windows operating system

_______________________ 25. the software program, such as Windows XP, that runs a computer

_______________________ 26. the use of the right mouse button to access special features of a
                             PC application

_______________________ 27. the X in the upper right corner of a window used to close a
                             document or an application window

_______________________ 28. the area of a computer's memory where temporary information is
                             stored

_______________________ 29. in a software application, a box that appears asking for a command
                             or input from the user

_______________________ 30. for software applications, such as word processing and
                             spreadsheet, this is the ability to share data; for example, using part
                             of a spreadsheet in a word processing document

_______________________ 31. the process of connecting data between files so that a change in
                             one will automatically cause a change in the other

_______________________ 32. in Microsoft Office, a set of buttons that are common in function in
                             the different applications, such as Word and Excel

Solutions to E-Mail Quick Check, page 37

1. e-mail attachment
2. emoticon
3. snail mail
4. Instant Messenger
5. SMTP
6. IMAP or POP3
7. IMAP
8. flame
9. e-mail group
10. e-mail
11. spam
12. list serve

Solutions to E-Term Quick Check, page 38

1. e-book
2. IT
3. e-term
4. e-business
5. e-paper
6. e-learning
7. IT
8. e-classes
9. online
10. telecommunications

Solutions to Hardware Quick Check, page 39

1. Pentium
2. NIC
3. Intel
4. infrared port
5. server
6. FireWire
7. PCMCIA
8. surge suppressor
9. UPS
10. Zip drive
11. scanner
12. DVD
13. Zip disk
14. adapter card
15. hub
16. router
17. GPS
18. modem
19. docking station
20. floppy disk
21. write-protect tab
22. PDA
23. hard drive
24. IEEE
25. CAT5
26. DRAM
27. ink-jet printer
28. laser printer
29. dot matrix printer
30. SDRAM
31. video card
32. sound card
33. dongle
34. flash card
35. GPS
36. Palm Pilot
37. CPU
38. VRAM
39. hardware
40. floppy drive
41. CD-ROM
42. Caps Lock
43. Num Lock
44. motherboard
45. microprocessor or processor
46. computer
47. laptop computer
48. mainframe
49. monitor
50. mouse
51. peripherals
52. supercomputer
53. tablet PC

Solutions to Internet Quick Check, page 42

1. JavaScript
2. Trojan horse
3. dot com
4. LAN party
5. web site
6. Internet filter
7. chat room
8. SSL

9. streaming
10. FTP
11. JavaScript error
12. intranet
13. Bulletin Board System
14. ISP
15. web page
16. cookie
17. HTML
18. denial of service
19. brick-and-mortar
20. worm
21. Shockwave
22. plug-in
23. Internet Explorer
24. Netscape
25. search engine
26. hyperlink
27. HTML
28. hypertext
29. virus
30. hypermedia
31. WWW
32. web address
33. Internet
34. HTTP
35. webmaster
36. log on
37. log in
38. upload
39. download
40. netiquette
41. home page
42. URL
43. browser
44. frames
45. web browser
46. web design

Solutions to Multimedia Quick Check, page 45

1. WAV
2. digital camera
3. animation
4. MP3
5. sound file
6. clip art
7. vector graphic
8. Dreamweaver
9. bitmap
10. transparent GIF
11. graphic
12. Fireworks
13. AVI
14. pixel
15. MIDI or MID
16. FreeHand
17. AIFF
18. AU
19. animated GIF
20. Macromedia Studio Suite
21. Media Player
22. Photoshop
23. JPEG or JPG
24. virtual reality
25. MIDI or MID
26. PCX
27. GIF
28. RA
29. BMP
30. MPEG or MPG
31. rip
32. multimedia

Solutions to Software Quick Check, page 47

1. record
2. database
3. absolute cell reference
4. C++
5. spreadsheet
6. Zip file
7. auto-format
8. program
9. software
10. Office
11. field
12. Boolean operators
13. cell address
14. FAQ
15. mail merge
16. OCR
17. cut and paste
18. data entry

19. CAD
20. computer-assisted instruction
21. PowerPoint
22. Excel
23. data type
24. FrontPage
25. Word
26. Works
27. drag and drop
28. Access
29. Outlook
30. unzip
31. query
32. word processing
33. functions
34. groupware
35. Quicken
36. voice recognition
37. ASCII
38. MOS
39. PageMaker
40. presentation software
41. ASCII
42. WYSIWYG
43. PDF
44. beta version
45. Publisher
46. Outlook Express
47. bug
48. Quark Xpress
49. copyright law
50. license
51. relational database
52. application
53. freeware
54. shareware
55. relative cell reference
56. slides
57. worksheet
58. shareware
59. Novell
60. word wrap
61. cell
62. desktop publishing
63. line break
64. shrink wrap license
65. header/footer

66. gutter
67. piracy
68. extension
69. orientation

Solutions to Technical Quick Check, page 51

1. terabyte
2. T-1
3. firewall
4. Ethernet
5. wireless
6. DSL
7. LCD
8. ISDN
9. MBPS
10. GHZ
11. GB
12. MHZ
13. dot pitch
14. PPM
15. USB
16. serial
17. parallel
18. MB
19. peer-to-peer
20. TCP/IP
21. TFT
22. PC
23. cache
24. offline
25. active matrix
26. digital
27. bidirectional
28. dpi
29. non-system disk error
30. resolution
31. proxy server
32. patch
33. LAN
34. K
35. ROM
36. RAM
37. WAN
38. LAN
39. network
40. IP

41. byte
42. bit
43. bps
44. boot
45. A+ certification
46. baud rate
47. compiler
48. help desk
49. Linux
50. PC repair
51. programming
52. protocol
53. security
54. Visual Basic

Solutions to Windows Quick Check, page 54

1. task bar
2. icon
3. tool bar
4. Ctrl key
5. Alt key
6. menu bar
7. drop-down menu
8. keyboard shortcut
9. scroll bar
10. sharing
11. shortcut
12. wizard
13. floating tool bar
14. dockable tool bar
15. Windows
16. Ctrl key
17. function keys
18. driver
19. maximize button
20. minimize button
21. restore button
22. Ctrl-Alt-Delete
23. path
24. desktop
25. operating system
26. right click
27. close button
28. Clipboard
29. dialog box
30. integration
31. linking
32. Smart Tags